bubblefacts...

AWESOME OCEANS

Miles KELLY
PUBLISHING

First published in 2005 by
Miles Kelly Publishing Ltd
Bardfield Centre, Great Bardfield, Essex, CM7 4SL

2 4 6 8 10 9 7 5 3 1

Publishing Director:
Anne Marshall

Cartoons:
Mark Davis

Editorial Assistant:
Hannah Todd

Designer:
Louisa Leitao

Senior Editor:
Belinda Gallagher

Production:
Estela Boulton

ISBN 1-84236-533-9

Printed in China

British Library Cataloguing-in-Publication Data
A catalogue record for this book is available from the British Library

Indexer: Jane Parker

www.mileskelly.net
info@mileskelly.net

Contents

Oceans cover more than two-thirds of Earth's surface.

Their total area is about 362 million square kilometres, which means there is more than twice as much ocean as land! Although all the oceans flow into each other, we know them as four different oceans – the Pacific, Atlantic, Indian and Arctic. Our landmasses, the continents, rise out of them.

The deepest ocean is the Pacific. In places it is so deep that Mount Everest would sink without a trace.

A sea is a small part of an ocean. For example, the Red Sea is the part of the Indian Ocean between Egypt and Saudi Arabia. Asia's Dead Sea isn't a true sea, but a landlocked lake. We call it a sea because it is a large body of water.

Ninety-seven percent of the world's water is in the oceans. Just a fraction is in freshwater lakes and rivers.

Oceans contain streams of water called currents. These can be strong and hard to swim against.

Ocean features

beneath the waves

There are plains, mountains and valleys under the oceans, in areas called basins. Each basin has a rim and sides. Inside there are vast flat plains, steep hills, huge underwater volcanoes called seamounts and deep valleys called trenches.

Liquid rock inside the Earth seeps out of holes in the seabed. This forms new layers of ocean floor.

Sometimes, a ring-shaped coral reef called an atoll marks where an island once was. The coral reef built up around the island. After the volcano blew its top, the reef remained.

The world's longest mountain chain is under the ocean. It is the Mid-ocean range and stretches around the middle of the Earth.

New islands form when layers of lava build up from underwater volcanoes.

Life on the rocks

limpet power!

Rock pools are teeming with all kinds of creatures. Limpets, sponges and anemones all attach themselves to rocks, stopping the waves washing them away. They eat scraps of food washed in with the tide. These pools are also the perfect place for crabs to find food and hide.

Some anemones shoot tiny hooks at each other. Hermit crabs use shells to protect their soft bodies.

Limpets are a kind of shellfish. They live on rocks and in pools at shorelines. Here, they eat slimy, green algae, but they have to withstand the crashing tide. They cling to the rock with their muscular foot, only moving when the tide is out.

Hermit crabs do not have shells. Most crabs shed their shells as they outgrow them, but the hermit crab does not have a shell. It borrows the leftover shell of a dead whelk or other mollusc – whatever it can squeeze into to protect its soft body. These crabs have even been spotted using a coconut shell as a home!

Green sea urchins disguise themselves to hide from predators. Sea sponges are simple living creatures.

Fins and tails

going swimmingly

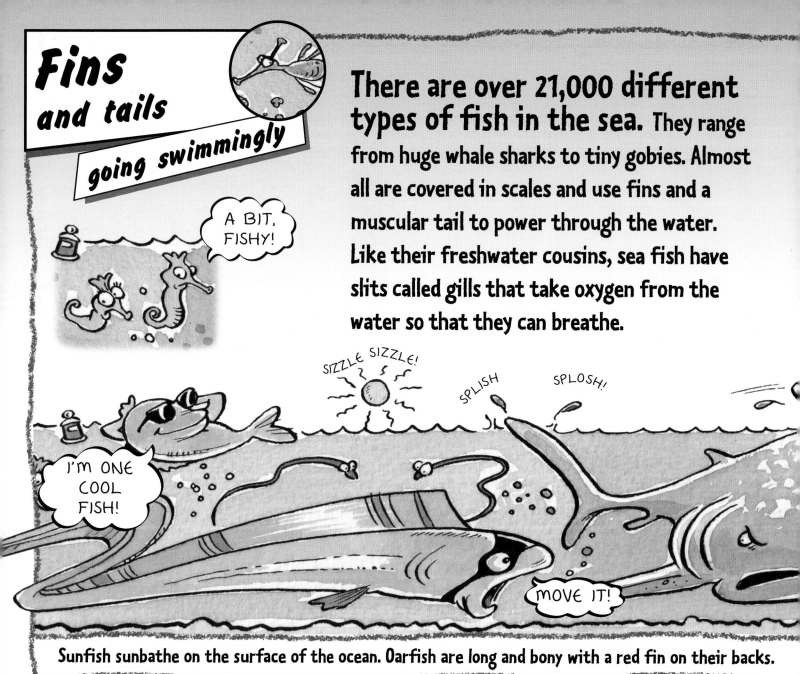

There are over 21,000 different types of fish in the sea. They range from huge whale sharks to tiny gobies. Almost all are covered in scales and use fins and a muscular tail to power through the water. Like their freshwater cousins, sea fish have slits called gills that take oxygen from the water so that they can breathe.

A BIT, FISHY!

SIZZLE SIZZLE!

SPLISH

SPLOSH!

I'M ONE COOL FISH!

MOVE IT!

Sunfish sunbathe on the surface of the ocean. Oarfish are long and bony with a red fin on their backs.

can you believe it?

Eels and salmon swim thousands of kilometres from the sea to spawn in the same river where they were born.

Fish can come in all shapes and sizes. Flounders and other flatfish have squashed, flat bodies. Eels are so long and thin that the biggest types look like snakes, while tiny garden eels resemble worms. Seahorses and seadragons look nothing like fish at all!

MAKE ME, FIN FACE!

SHARK ALERT!

JUST A FLYING VISIT!

BUBBLE!

BUBBLE!

Flying fish do not fly, but leap. The flounder's shape and colours help to camouflage it on the seabed.

Super sharks

teeth and jaws

Great whites are the scariest sharks in the oceans. These powerful predators have been known to kill people and can speed through the water at 30 kilometres an hour. Unlike most fish, the great white is warm-blooded. This allows its muscles to work well, but it also means that the shark has to feed on plenty of meat.

Great white sharks will attack and eat almost anything, but they prefer to feed on seals.

Most sharks are meat-eaters. Strangely, some of the biggest sharks eat the smallest prey. Huge whale sharks and basking sharks eat tiny sea creatures called plankton.

The skin of the cookie-cutter shark glows in the dark to attract prey.

ALL THE BETTER TO SEE YOU WITH!

BEDTIME FOR LITTLE SHARKS.

EYES AT THE BACK... I MEAN SIDE OF YOUR HEAD!

OH MUM!

GULP!

Hammerheads prey on other sharks. Tiger sharks have as many as 40 pups that fend for themselves.

Whale watch

friendly giants

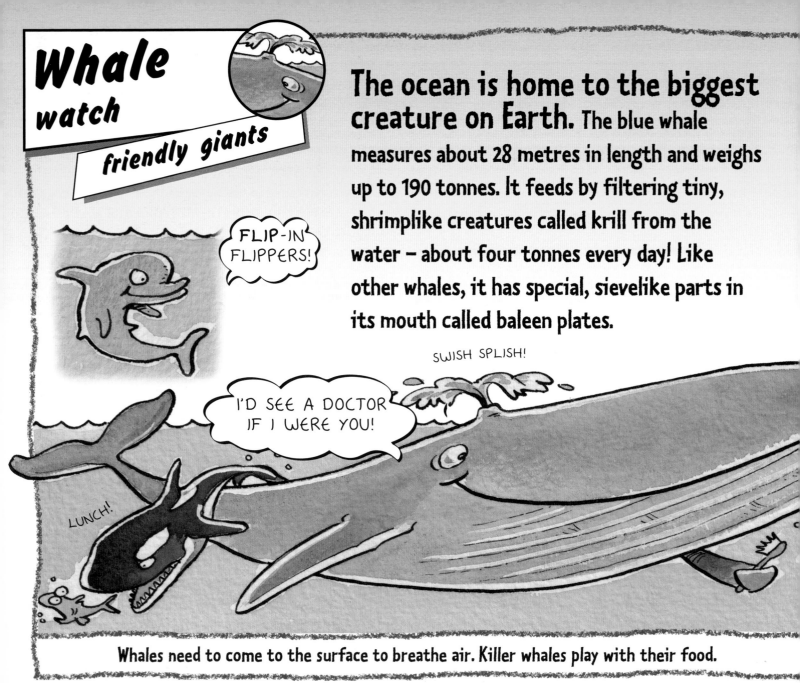

The ocean is home to the biggest creature on Earth. The blue whale measures about 28 metres in length and weighs up to 190 tonnes. It feeds by filtering tiny, shrimplike creatures called krill from the water – about four tonnes every day! Like other whales, it has special, sievelike parts in its mouth called baleen plates.

FLIP-IN FLIPPERS!

SWISH SPLISH!

I'D SEE A DOCTOR IF I WERE YOU!

LUNCH!

Whales need to come to the surface to breathe air. Killer whales play with their food.

Leopard seals, found in the Antarctic, chirp and whistle while they snooze.

Dolphins and whales sing songs to communicate. The noisiest is the humpback whale, whose wailing noises can be heard for hundreds of kilometres. The sweetest is the beluga – nicknamed the 'sea canary'. Songs are used to attract a mate, or just to keep track of each other.

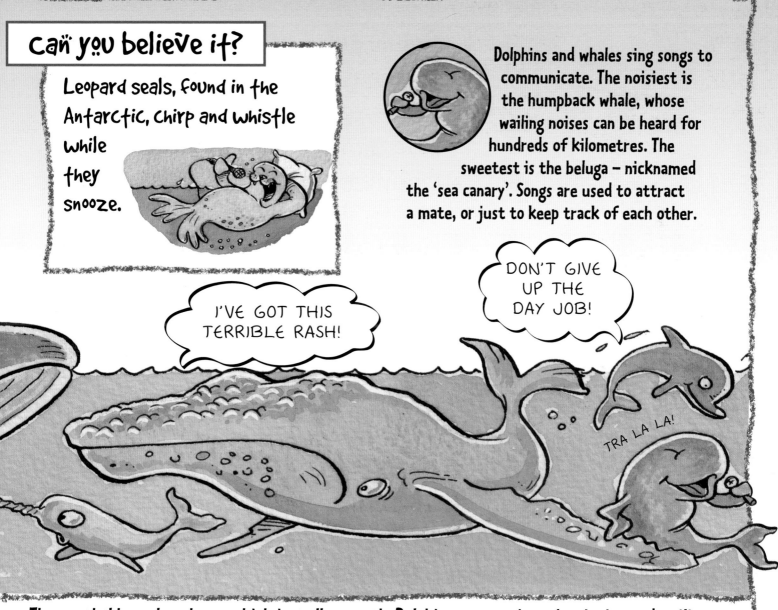

I'VE GOT THIS TERRIBLE RASH!

DON'T GIVE UP THE DAY JOB!

TRA LA LA!

The narwhal has a long horn, which is really a tooth. Dolphins communicate by singing and wailing.

Deep down below
the icy depths

Few creatures can survive in the icy-cold ocean depths. Food is so hard to come by, the deep-sea anglerfish does not waste energy chasing prey – it has developed a clever fishing trick. A stringy 'fishing rod' with a glowing tip extends from its dorsal fin or hangs above its jaw. This attracts smaller fish to the anglerfish's big mouth.

Only the glowing fishing rod is visible of an anglerfish. The lantern fish's whole body glows in the dark.

Some deep-sea fish glow in the dark. As well as tempting prey, light also confuses predators. About 1500 different deep-sea fish give off light. The lantern fish's whole body glows, while the dragon fish has light organs along its sides and belly.

Cookie-cutter sharks take biscuit-shaped bites out of their prey. These strange, deep water sharks are only 50 centimetres long. Instead of eating whole animals, they attach themselves to their prey by sucking with their mouths. They then swivel their sharp teeth round in a circle, removing a lump of flesh.

IT'S THE COOKIE MONSTER!

SO, MY REPUTATION PRECEDES ME!

EEK!

CHOMP!

OH!

JAW WARS!

Black swallowers unhinge their jaws to fit food in. Viperfish have teeth that are invisible in the dark.

Coral capers

Tiny animals build huge underwater walls. These are built up from coral, the leftover skeletons of sea creatures called polyps. Over millions of years, enough skeletons pile up to form huge, wall-like structures called reefs. Coral reefs are full of hidey-holes and make brilliant habitats for all sorts of amazing, colourful sea life.

Parrot fish

Seahorse

Giant clam

Clown fish

Male seahorses store their eggs in a pouch. When the young are ready to hatch they swim out into the ocean

The clownfish is sting-proof. Most creatures steer clear of an anemone's stinging tentacles, but the clownfish swims among the stingers, where it's safe from predators. The anemone doesn't seem to sting the clownfish.

Lion fish

Cleaner wrasse fish

Stone fish

Clownfish are immune to the sting of anemones. Stone fish are well camouflaged on the seabed.

Perfect penguins
on the ice

Macaroni, chinstrap, and emperor are all penguins. There are 17 different types, and most live around the Antarctic. Penguins feed on fish, squid and krill. Their black-and-white plumage is important camouflage. Seen from above, a penguin's black back blends in with the water.

Penguins can swim but they cannot fly. They have oily waterproofed feathers and flipper-like wings.

Gentoo penguins build nests out of stone circles on the shingled shores where they breed.

The male emperor penguin keeps his egg warm on his feet. The female returns when the chick hatches.

First voyages across the sea

The first boats were made from tree trunks. Early people hollowed out tree trunks to craft their own dug-outs. For several hundred years, the Maori people of New Zealand made log war canoes, decorating them with beautiful carvings.

Greek warships were rowed by three layers of oarsmen. A painted eye was believed to protect from evil.

The 1400s were an amazing time of exploration and discovery. One English explorer, Christopher Columbus, set sail from Spain in 1492 with a fleet of three ships. He hoped to find a new trade route to India, but instead he found the Americas!

Barnacles are shellfish that attach themselves to ships' hulls, or even whales!

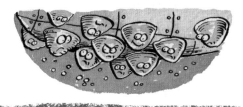

DON'T YOU WAVE YOUR FIST AT ME!

YES! AMERICA AT LAST

Vikings decorated their boats to scare enemies. Columbus' most famous ship was the *Santa Maria*.

Pirate plunder

pieces of eight

Pirates once ruled the high seas. Pirates attack and board other ships to steal their cargoes. Their golden age was during the 1600s and 1700s. This was when heavily laden ships carried treasure, weapons and goods back to Europe from colonies in the Americas, Africa and Asia.

LET'S SHIVER THEIR TIMBERS!

GOTCHA!

GERONIMO!

EEK!

BUNCH OF WIMPS!

There were women pirates, too. They wore men's clothes and fought with daggers and pistols.

can you believe it?

There is treasure lying under the sea! over the centuries, ships sunk in storms. They include pirate ships loaded with booty.

Edward Teach, better known as Blackbeard, was one of the most terrifying pirates. He attacked ships off the coast of North America during the early 1700s. To frighten his victims, it is said that he used to set fire to his own beard!

Luxury yachts are still a target for pirates. The bed of the Caribbean Sea has remains of rich galleons.

Ocean harvests
watery treasure

Oysters come from beds! To gather oysters, fishermen rear them on trays or poles in the water. First, they collect oyster larvae, or babies. They attract them with sticks hung with shells.

Adult lobsters are caught in pots. Oyster larvae are attracted to fishing sticks.

Sea minerals, such as oil and gas, are useful substances that are pumped to shore to be used as fuel.

Salt is collected from dried sea water. Pearls are made when a grain of sand is lodged in an oyster shell.

Riding the waves
surfer's paradise

Surfing was the first sea sport.
It took off in the 1950s, but was invented centuries earlier in Hawaii. At Waimea Bay in Hawaii, surfers catch waves that are up to 11 metres high. The longest rides, though, are made off the coast of Mexico, where it is possible to surf for more than 1.5 kilometres.

In 1986, off the coast of Australia, a world record was set when 100 waterskiers were towed by one boat.

People said *Titanic* was unsinkable. But it hit an iceberg and sank on its maiden voyage.

Three hulls are sometimes better than one. Powerboating is an exciting, dangerous sport. Competitors are always trying out new boat designs that will race even faster. Trimarans have three slender, streamlined hulls that cut through the water.

SPLASH!

I'M NO DRAG!

Z O O O O O O O O O m !

WELL I'm A HIGH FLYER!

Multi-hulled boats minimize drag. Hydroplanes have 'wings' that raise the hull above the water.

Ocean stories

myth and legend

The Greek hero Jason made an epic sea voyage. In the legend of the Argonauts, a hero called Jason sets off in a boat called the *Argos* with a band of brave men. He goes on a quest to find the Golden Fleece, a precious sheepskin guarded by a fierce dragon.

NEPTUNE'S HAVING A BAD DAY!

Greeks and Romans both believed that there was a god who ruled the seas, called Neptune or Poseidon.

Mermaids lured sailors to their deaths on the rocks. Mythical mermaids were said to be half-women, half-fish. Folklore tells how they confused sailors with their beautiful singing – with the result that sailors' ships were wrecked on the rocks.

Aprhrodite, the Greek goddess of love, was born in the sea. The Romans based their love goddess Venus on the same story.

YUMMY! TIME FOR A SNACK!

SWOON!

HELLOOO THERE!

People once believed in a sea monster called the kraken, now thought to be mistaken for a giant squid.

Index